P9-CCB-789

GREAT WHITE SHARK
Ruler of the Sea

SMITHSONIAN OCEANIC COLLECTION

To Geoffrey — K.W.Z.

For Alissa Ann and Joseph John with love. — S.J.P.

Book Design: Shields & Partners, Westport, CT

First Edition 1995
10 9 8 7 6
Printed in China

Acknowledgements:
   Our very special thanks to Dr. Victor G. Springer of the Department of Vertebrate Zoology
at the Smithsonian's National Museum of Natural History for his curatorial review.

GREAT WHITE SHARK
Ruler of the Sea

by Kathleen Weidner Zoehfeld   Illustrated by Steven James Petruccio

Soundprints
Where Children Discover Nature

G reat white sharks move in from all directions to feast on the carcass of a dead whale. Heads up and teeth flashing, they rip huge chunks of meat from the whale's sides.

From a mile away, White Shark hears the commotion. She picks up the scent of food and swims in quickly, driven by hunger.

She is two days old, and from the moment of her birth, she has been on her own. Great white shark mothers do not stay to feed their young, and they do not teach them how to scavenge or hunt. White Shark did not need to be taught. She was born knowing.

With a flick of her crescent tail, she launches her strong, four-foot body through the mob of feeding sharks. She opens her mouth, ready for a bite of whale meat.

8

At that moment, a seventeen-foot adult bumps into White Shark and throws her off course. She snaps her jaws shut on — nothing. Frustrated, she turns back for another try.

Great white sharks many times her size gorge themselves, leaving only a few crumbs for White Shark.

She dives toward the bottom, where she gobbles up one crab — two crabs — three crabs.

Still hungry, she hunts the vast ocean, alone. Alert.

In the distance, she hears a low fluttering sound. Instinct tells her it may be an easy meal — an injured fish. But first she must find it.

She zig-zags through the water, listening for the direction of the sound. Soon her keen nose smells food. Her tail twitches, and she begins to swim faster. She follows the scent of her prey like a bloodhound.

13

Up ahead, a school of white seabass move in unison.
Their silvery sides flash like coins in the sun.
One fish struggles to keep up with the school, its
ragged tail fluttering. White Shark spots it.

15

She zeroes in. With a few quick thrusts of her tail, she speeds up —
five, ten, fifteen miles an hour.

Suddenly, her mouth gapes open, and her eyes roll back in her head to protect them from injury when she snaps up her prey.

With sharp, triangle-teeth she clamps down.

But just as White Shark bites, a swordfish flies at the seabass, trying to seize it for himself.

He is too late for the fish, but he cannot stop himself from colliding headlong into White Shark. His sword grazes her thick, rough skin. She is injured, but the seabass is hers.

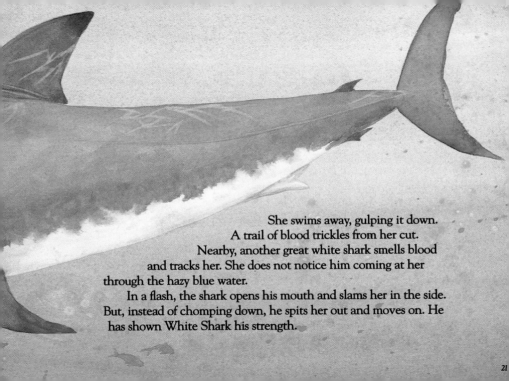

She swims away, gulping it down.
A trail of blood trickles from her cut.
Nearby, another great white shark smells blood
and tracks her. She does not notice him coming at her
through the hazy blue water.
In a flash, the shark opens his mouth and slams her in the side.
But, instead of chomping down, he spits her out and moves on. He
has shown White Shark his strength.

Stunned and wounded, White Shark cannot swim any farther. She slowly sinks to the bottom.

No mother comes to protect her. No one urges her on. But she was born strong. By instinct she knows she must swim, or she will die. From deep within, she summons the will to keep moving.

Over many days, her wounds begin to heal. The seabass sustains her for a while. But soon, hunger is gnawing at her again.

She weaves silently through a forest of kelp, searching for food.

In the distance, a huge white shark looms toward her. He is even bigger than the shark that wounded her. But this time she is watching. She dodges out of his way.

Then, just below the shimmering, sunlit surface, she spots a sea lion playing. The sea lion sees her too, and he taunts her. She charges after him. The sea lion ducks behind a rock, and she cannot find him. She gnashes her teeth in frustration.

The sea lion is too much for her now. She must find easier prey.

Undaunted, White Shark moves out into deeper waters. She discovers a school of tuna and stalks them. Soon she slices a bite out of a large straggler.

A group of hungry pilot fish gather around and pick off the tuna crumbs. White Shark feels her strength returning.

From now on, pilot fish stay with her wherever she goes. They depend on her hunting skills for their food. In return, they are her servants, tidying up after her every meal.

Month after month White Shark hunts. Her teeth grow wider and stronger. Her sleek, gray body grows longer and stouter. Month after month she grows more powerful, more skillful at the hunt.

After many years, she reaches her full
size — twenty feet long and four thousand
pounds. Now, smaller sharks scoot out of her way.
Swordfish give her a wide berth. Sea lions do not taunt her
anymore. Fish of every shape and size scatter in her wake and hide.
She is White Shark, ruler of the sea.

31

About the Great White Shark

Great white sharks are white only on their bellies. Individual great whites vary from light gray to black on their backs. They live near coasts as well as offshore, mainly in cool or temperate waters. The biggest white shark ever measured was 21 feet long, weighing over 4,800 pounds. White sharks are the largest hunting-fish in the sea. Adults are strong enough to attack animals as huge as the 8,000-pound northern elephant seals. But a hungry white shark will rarely turn down an easy meal, such as a dead or injured fish.

Scientists know very little about the lives of great white sharks. Exactly how do they use their senses to hunt? Do they migrate? Where and how are baby whites born? These and many other questions remain to be answered.

One important question now is: are white sharks in danger of becoming extinct? Scientists are working hard to learn more about the ways of the white shark, so they can help prevent it from being endangered.

Glossary

carcass: The body of a dead animal.

crab: A sea creature with claws and a rounded body covered by an armor-like shell.

instinct: A knowledge or type of behavior an animal inherits from its parents. Instinctive behavior does not have to be learned.

kelp: A brown seaweed that grows in cool, rocky, coastal waters.

pilot fish: A small banded fish that often swims with sharks.

scavenge: To feed on the remains of a dead animal.

school: A group of fish of the same type swimming together.

sea lion: A large, brown seal living in the sea and on shore.

swordfish: A large hunting-fish with a long, sharp upper jaw, which it uses to strike its prey.

tuna: A large, fast-swimming fish with a deep iridescent blue back and a silver-white belly.

whale: A huge, air-breathing sea mammal.

white seabass: A spiny-finned schooling fish with steel-blue tops and silvery sides.